FLANNEL MAN CANDY COOKBOOK

By Tim Murphy

Second Edition

Copyright 2016
Shamrock Arrow Media

For information on Flannel John's Cookbooks for Guys, upcoming releases and merchandise visit www.flanneljohn.com

FLANNEL JOHN'S MAN CANDY COOKBOOK

Bacon. It truly is man candy. That salty, sweet, smoky, succulent, savory meat harvested from pigs. It's enough to convert a full-fledged vegan into a drooling carnivore. At one time it was a humble breakfast staple or one-third of a B.L.T. Bacon has evolved…as candy, dessert, appetizer, flavoring, main course and beyond. You can weave it, crumble it, coat it, shred it and…eat it. It's the culinary equivalent of Play Doh. You can make it into anything you want. This book has become so popular in the Flannel John series that I've assembled a second edition and expanded it with more bacon-inspired dishes. Indulge and enjoy.

Tim Murphy - Author

TABLE OF CONTENTS

Bacon Almond Cheese Dip_____Page 7
Bacon & Eggs Breakfast Pie_____Page 8
Bacon Barbecue Burger_____Page 9
Bacon, Bean & Wiener Hot Dish_____Page 10
Bacon Burgers_____Page 11
Bacon Butter_____Page 12
Bacon Cheddar Corn Bread_____Page 13
Bacon Cheese BBQ Hot Dogs_____Page 14
Bacon Monkey Bread_____Page 15
Bacon Roll-Ups_____Page 16
Bacon-Wrapped Scallops_____Page 17
Bacon-Wrapped Sesame Sticks_____Page 18
Bacon-Wrapped Tater Tots_____Page 19
Baked Beans_____Page 20
Baked Oysters_____Page 21
Bean & Bacon Soup_____Page 22
Beef, Bacon, Sausage & Beans_____Page 23
Beef Jerky & Bacon Chili_____Page 24
Beer, Cheese & Bacon Soup_____Page 25
Big Island Barbecue Burger_____Page 26
Blazing Saddles Baked Beans_____Page 27
BLT Burger_____Page 28
Bread Bowl Bacon Dip_____Page 29
Breakfast Bacon Pie_____Page 30
Brown Sugar & Maple Bacon_____Page 31
California Clam Chowder_____Page 32

Candied Maple Bacon	Page 33
Cheese & Bacon English Muffins	Page 34
Cheese & Bacon Popcorn	Page 35
Cheeseburger Deluxe	Page 36
Chocolate Painted Bacon	Page 37
Cluck & Oink Burger	Page 38
Clam Chowder	Page 39
Corn Chowder	Page 40
Crabmeat & Bacon Rolls	Page 41
Crispy Bacon Oysters	Page 42
Fiesta Burger	Page 43
Fish Stew	Page 44
Glazed Bacon	Page 45
Great White North Bacon Soup	Page 46
Ham & Bacon Fried Rice	Page 47
Heart Stopping Weenies	Page 48
Hot Bacon & Cheese Dip	Page 49
Hunters Feast	Page 50
Northwest Passage Chowder	Page 51
Nuts & Bacon	Page 52
Quacker and Bacon	Page 53
Split Pea Soup	Page 54
Stuffed Mushrooms	Page 55
Sweet & Spicy Bacon	Page 56
Trout With an Oink	Page 57
Twisted Bacon	Page 58
Venison Bacon Burgers	Page 59
Wild Rice & Bacon Soup	Page 60

BACON ALMOND CHEESE DIP

1 pound of Cheddar cheese, shredded
12 green onions, diced
1 pound of bacon, cooked and crumbled
2 cups of mayonnaise or Miracle Whip
1 cup of almonds, slivered and toasted
Salt to taste

Mix all ingredients thoroughly and chill for at least 4 hours. Serve with crackers on vegetables.

BACON & EGGS BREAKFAST PIE

10 strips of bacon
6 eggs
3 tablespoons of milk
½ teaspoon of salt
Dash of pepper

Arrange 10 slices of cooked (but not crisp) bacon to cover the bottom and sides of an 8-inch pie plate. Beat together eggs, milk, salt and pepper. Pour mixture in the pie plate and bake at 375 degrees for 30 minutes.

BACON BARBECUE BURGER

½ pound of ground beef
¼ cup of barbecue sauce
2 pineapple rings
4 strips of bacon
2 hamburger buns
Salt and pepper to taste

Combine ground beef with barbecue sauce and mix thoroughly. Season meat with salt and pepper. Form into 2 patties. Grill or broil for 4 to 6 minutes per side. Grill pineapple rings for 4 minutes. In a separate skillet, cook bacon until crispy. Top each meat patty with a pineapple ring and 2 pieces of bacon. Serve on toasted buns.

BACON, BEAN & WIENER HOT DISH

½ pound of diced bacon
6 hot dogs sliced into 1-inch pieces
¼ cup of chopped onion
¼ cup of chopped green pepper
¾ cup of pineapple chunks, drained
1 cup of catsup
2 tablespoons of Worcestershire sauce
1 large can of drained pork and beans
  (30 ounces)

Fry bacon until crisp then add hot dogs, onion, pepper and pineapple. Cook until onion is tender then add remaining ingredients. Bake at 300 degrees uncovered for 1 hour.

BACON BURGERS

1½ pounds of bacon
Barbecue sauce or ketchup (optional)
Hamburger buns

Put bacon into a blender or food processor and pulse to chop. When it reaches the right consistency, form into 5 or 6 thin patties. If mixture is a little dry, you can stir in a tablespoon or two of barbecue sauce or ketchup to hold it together. Cook in a pan over medium heat, about 8 to 10 minutes per side. Serve on toasted buns.

BACON BUTTER

1 stick of butter, softened
2 strips of bacon
2 tablespoons of maple syrup

Fry bacon in a pan and reserve the drippings. Chop bacon into very small pieces. Blend butter with the drippings and maple syrup. Once thoroughly blended, stir in bacon.

BACON CHEDDAR CORN BREAD

1 cup of flour
¼ cup sugar
2 teaspoons baking powder
1 teaspoon of baking soda
½ teaspoon salt
1¼ cups yellow corn meal
1½ cups low-fat or regular buttermilk
1 large egg
1 cup grated sharp cheddar cheese
5 ounces cooked bacon in small pieces
   (4 to 6 slices)
2 tablespoons unsalted butter, melted
Softened butter for greasing pan

Sift flour, sugar, baking powder, baking soda and salt into a bowl. Add cornmeal and mix well. Mix buttermilk, egg and butter in a separate bowl. Pour flour mixture over buttermilk mixture and stir slowly until combined. Add bacon and cheese and stir. Pour into a lightly greased 9-inch pan and bake at 400 degrees for about 20 minutes. After it cools, slice into squares.

BACON CHEESE BBQ HOT DOGS

8 hot dogs
8 hot dog buns
8 slices of cheddar cheese
8 slices of bacon
½ cup of barbecue sauce
1 red onion, diced

Place bacon in a deep skillet. Cook over medium-high heat until browned and drain on paper towels. In a separate pan or on a barbecue, grill hot dogs cook browned and fully cooked, or until done to your taste. Lightly toast or grill hot dog buns. Now place a slice of cheese and bacon on each roll. Add a hot dog and top each with 1 tablespoon of barbecue sauce and red onion.

BACON MONKEY BREAD

12 strips of bacon, shredded
1 loaf of frozen bread dough, thawed
2 tablespoons of olive oil (or vegetable oil)
4 cups of shredded mozzarella
1 envelope of ranch salad dressing mix

Shred bacon and cook for 5 minutes or until slightly under done then drain on paper towels. Divide dough into one-inch pieces, roll into balls and place in a large bowl. Add 1 tablespoon of oil to coat. Add in bacon, cheese, dressing mix and remaining oil. Toss to coat dough. Arrange pieces on a greased baking sheet. Cover and let rise for 30 minutes until doubling in size. Bake at 350 degrees for 15 minutes. Cover with foil and bake 5 to 10 minutes longer or until brown.

BACON ROLL-UPS

½ cup of sour cream
½ teaspoon of onion salt
½ pound of bacon, cooked and crumbled
1 package of crescent rolls (8 ounce size)

Mix sour cream, onion salt and bacon then spread on the rolls and roll them up. Bake at 375 degrees for 12 to 15 minutes.

BACON-WRAPPED SCALLOPS

24 scallops
12 slices of bacon
Toothpicks

Cut bacon slices in half. Wrap a slice around each scallop and secure with a toothpick. Broil for 4 minutes, turn, and broil for an additional 4 minutes. You want them to be crisp, not burnt.

BACON-WRAPPED SESAME STICKS

    24 sesame sticks, 4 to 5 inches long
    12 slices of bacon
    1 cup of Parmesan cheese
    2 teaspoons of garlic salt

Cut bacon slices in half and wrap each one around a sesame stick. Place on a cookie sheet and bake at 350 degrees for 30 minutes. Remove from oven and sprinkle with cheese while hot.

BACON-WRAPPED TATER TOTS

24 tater tots
12 slices of bacon
Toothpicks

Cut bacon strips in half. Wrap each bacon piece tightly around a tater tot and secure with a toothpick. Place tater tots on a cookie sheet and bake at 425 degrees for 15 to 20 minutes.

BAKED BEANS

3 cans of pork and beans
3 pieces of bacon
½ of a large onion, chopped
½ cup of brown sugar
1/3 cup of molasses
1 teaspoon of mustard
Pinch of salt and pepper

Cook bacon and crumble into small pieces. Mix all ingredients in a 9-inch by 13-inch pan. Cover and bake at 250 degrees for 3 hours.

BAKED OYSTERS

1 pint of oysters
12 slices of half-cooked bacon
6 ounces of whole mushrooms, canned
1 green pepper, cut in squares
4 tablespoons of margarine, melted
1 tablespoon of lemon juice
¼ teaspoon of salt
Pepper to taste
Garlic powder to taste

Wrap oysters in bacon. Place on skewers and alternate with mushrooms and green pepper squares. Place in a baking dish. Combine remaining ingredients and brush on oysters. Bake at 450 degrees for 10 minutes.

BEAN & BACON SOUP

1 pound of beans
4 slices of chopped bacon
1 chopped onion
2 stalks of celery, chopped
3 quarts of water
½ tablespoon of sugar
Salt and pepper

Soak beans overnight in water. Fry bacon until it's crisp, remove and drain. Add beans, bacon, water, onion, celery and sugar. Simmer for about 3 hours.

BEEF, BACON, SAUSAGE & BEANS

1 pound of ground beef, browned
½ pound of polish sausage
5 slices of bacon
1 large onion, chopped
¼ cup of brown sugar
1½ tablespoons of Worcestershire sauce
1 small can of tomato sauce
1 large can of baked beans

Cut bacon into 1-inch pieces and cook until crisp. Drain grease and add onion and sausage. Cook until onion is sautéed. Drain. In a separate bowl, mix beans, brown sugar, tomato sauce and Worcestershire sauce. Stir until completely blended. Add in the meat and mix well. Bake in a greased casserole dish at 350 degrees for 20 to 25 minutes.

BEEF JERKY & BACON CHILI

½ cup of chopped bacon
1 onion, chopped
2 cloves of garlic, minced
2 cups beef broth
4 chili peppers, chopped
2 tablespoons chili powder
2 tablespoons light brown sugar
1½ tablespoons of cumin
5 cups fresh tomatoes, peeled & chopped
½ tablespoon pepper
2½ cups of beef jerky, chopped
2½ cups kidney or pinto beans, cooked

Cook bacon in deep pot or Dutch oven until fat is released, but not crisp. Add onion and garlic and cook until tender. Add in chili peppers, tomatoes and broth. Cook until tomatoes are soft, 15 to 20 minutes. Now combine chili powder, brown sugar, cumin and pepper and then add to pot. Stir in the beef jerky. Simmer or low boil for 45 minutes. Add beans and boil for about 5 minutes.

BEER, CHEESE & BACON SOUP

3 slices of bacon, in pieces
½ cup of green onion, chopped
2 tablespoons of flour
1 can of cream of chicken soup
8 ounces of shredded Cheddar cheese
12 ounces of beer
1 cup of milk

Fry bacon until slightly crisp. Add onion and sauté until tender. Remove from heat and stir in flour. Add soup and heat until boiling. Stir in cheese until melted. Add beer and milk until foam disappears and soup is hot. Do not boil.

BIG ISLAND BARBECUE BURGER

½ pound of ground beef
¼ cup of barbecue sauce
2 pineapple rings
4 strips of bacon
2 hamburger buns
Salt and pepper to taste

Combine ground beef with barbecue sauce and mix thoroughly. Season meat with salt and pepper. Form into 2 patties. Grill or broil for 4 to 6 minutes per side. Grill pineapple rings for 4 minutes. In a separate skillet, cook bacon until crispy. Top each meat patty with a pineapple ring and 2 pieces of bacon. Serve on toasted buns.

BLAZING SADDLES BAKED BEANS

5 slices of bacon, shredded into small pieces
1 large onion, diced
1 large can baked beans
1/3 cup of brown sugar
1/2 cup of ketchup

Cook bacon and onion until onion is soft and meat is mostly cooked without being crisp. Drain grease. Mix in remaining ingredients thoroughly. Bake mixture at 350 degrees for 60 minutes.

BLT BURGER

1 pound of ground steak
½ pound of bacon, diced
1 onion, grated
3 cloves of garlic, crushed
2 teaspoons of oil
Tomato, sliced
Lettuce
4 hamburger buns

Mix bacon, steak, garlic and onion thoroughly together. Form into 4 patties and place in a refrigerator for 1 hour. Add oil to a skillet and heat. Cook each burger for 4 to 6 minutes per side or to desired doneness. Top with lettuce and tomato.

BREAD BOWL BACON DIP

1 loaf of round Italian bread, unsliced
6 slices of bacon, cooked and crumbled
8 ounces of Monterey Jack cheese, shredded
4 ounces of Parmesan cheese, shredded
¼ cup of onion, diced
1 cup of mayonnaise
1 clove of garlic, minced

Cut the top third of the loaf of bread off and hollow out the remainder leaving a 1-inch shell. Combine remaining ingredients and carefully scoop into the bread bowl. Place on a cookie sheet. Bake at 350 degrees for 1 hour or until mixture is thoroughly heated.

BREAKFAST BACON PIE

12 slices of bacon, fried and crumbled
1 cup shredded cheese, Swiss or cheddar
¼ cup chopped onion
1 cup Bisquick
1/8 teaspoon of pepper
4 eggs
2 cups milk
¼ teaspoon salt

Lightly grease pie plate. Sprinkle bacon, cheese and onion in pie plate. Beat remaining ingredients until smooth. Pour evenly into pie plate. Bake at 400 degrees for 35 minutes. Let stand for 5 minutes before cutting.

BROWN SUGAR & MAPLE BACON

1 pound of bacon, thick-cut
4 tablespoons of brown sugar
2 tablespoons of maple syrup
Oil

Place a baking rack on a cookie sheet. Lightly brush oil on the rack. Line up bacon strips on the rack but don't let them touch. Combine brown sugar and syrup and warm in the microwave. Brush the warm mixture on the bacon. Bake at 350 degrees for 30 to 35 minutes.

CALIFORNIA CLAM CHOWDER

6 clams, finely chopped (save clam juice)
¼ pound of bacon
1 quart of milk
2½ cups of potatoes, diced
2 cups of boiling water
2 onions, diced
2 tablespoons of butter
½ cup of celery, diced
¼ teaspoon of white pepper
½ teaspoon of salt
Cornstarch (optional)

In a skillet, fry bacon until crisp and add onions. Sauté for 5 minutes. Add celery, potatoes and seasonings. Add water, cover, and simmer for 20 minutes. Add clams, clam juice, followed by milk and butter. Heat and stir. Thicken with cornstarch if you like. Keep stirring until creamy and hot.

CANDIED MAPLE BACON

1 pound of bacon, thick-cut
½ cup of maple syrup
1 teaspoon of Dijon mustard
Ground black pepper

Place a baking rack on a cookie sheet. Line up bacon strips on the rack but don't let them touch. Mix together syrup, mustard and pepper and spoon over bacon. Put the rack and cookie sheet in the oven and bake at 400 degrees for 12 minutes. Turn slices and baste with mixture again for 5 to 10 minutes until reaching desired doneness.

CHEESE & BACON ENGLISH MUFFINS

6 English muffins
8 slices of bacon, shredded
2¼ cups of Cheddar cheese, shredded
¼ cup of ketchup

Combine cheese, bacon and ketchup thoroughly. Spread over the 12 halves of the English muffins. Place on a baking sheet or oven rack. Broil or bake on low in the oven until the bacon is cooked. Be careful not to burn the muffins.

CHEESE & BACON POPCORN

5 cups of popped corn
4 tablespoons of bacon, cooked and crumbled
3 teaspoons of bacon drippings
¼ cup of Cheddar cheese, grated fine
¼ cup of Parmesan cheese

Fry the bacon and reserve the grease. Pop the corn and it drizzle it with the drippings. Mix thoroughly and toss with crumbled bacon. Shake cheese over the popcorn and toss again.

CHEESEBURGER DELUXE

1 pound of ground beef
8 slices of bacon
1 onion
2 cloves of garlic, crushed
2 teaspoons of grated horseradish
4 slices of American or Cheddar cheese
2 tablespoons of oil
Pepper
4 hamburger buns

Finely dice 1 onion and mix with ground beef. Now add garlic, horseradish and pepper to the meat, mix thoroughly and shape into 4 patties. Wrap each patty in 2 slices of bacon, cover and chill for at least 60 minutes. Cook burgers in a skillet or a broiler for 4 to 5 minutes per side or to desired doneness. Top meat with cheese or cook for final minute with cheese on top of meat.

CHOCOLATE PAINTED BACON

12 slices of thick-cut bacon
12 wooden skewers
1 cup of semi-sweet chocolate chips
1 tablespoon of shortening

Thread each piece of bacon on to a skewer. Place baking rack on a cookie sheet and place bacon skewers on the rack. Bake at 400 degrees for 20 to 25 minutes until bacon is crisp. Remove from oven and let cool. Put chocolate and shortening in a microwave-safe bowl. Heat for 20 seconds spurts, stirring after each interval until mixture is completely smooth. Paint each bacon strip with chocolate and place on wax paper. Cool in the refrigerator for at least 1 hour.

CLUCK & OINK BURGER

1½ cups of chicken, ground or shredded
½ pound of bacon
6 shallots
2 garlic cloves
1 tablespoon of tomato paste
1 tablespoon of parsley
4 tablespoons of whole-wheat flour
2 tablespoons of oil
Salt and pepper to taste
4 hamburger buns

Bake or fry bacon until crisp. Drain and let cool. Place the bacon in a blender or food processor with chicken, shallots and garlic. Blend well. Add tomato paste, parsley and salt and pepper. Mix for 1 to 2 minutes. Form into 4 patties and dredge in flour. Cook in a skillet with oil or in a broiler for 5 to 6 minutes per side.

CLAM CHOWDER

3 dozen clams in their shells
3 cups of clam broth
4 slices of bacon
4 tablespoons of melted butter
2½ cups of raw, diced potatoes
4 cups of milk
2 tablespoons of flour
2 medium onions
Salt and pepper to taste
Water

Open clams and drain the liquid through cheesecloth. Grind clams. Fry up onions and bacon until brown. Combine clams, potatoes, bacon and onions. Add enough water to cook potatoes and clams. When finished, add clam liquid, milk and seasonings. Make a paste of melted butter and flour to thicken the mixture. Add butter, salt and pepper to taste.

CORN CHOWDER

4 slices of bacon
1 medium onion, chopped
1 can of chopped tomatoes
1 can of corn
1 tablespoon of sugar
3 cups of water
2½ cups of diced potatoes

Cook bacon until crisp. Add onion and sauté until limp, then drain. Add remaining ingredients and salt and pepper to taste then simmer for 25 minutes.

CRABMEAT & BACON ROLLS

1 cup of crabmeat
8 slices of bacon, cut in half
½ cup of fine dry bread crumbs
¼ cup of tomato juice
1 egg, well beaten
1 tablespoon of parsley, chopped
1 tablespoon of lemon juice
¼ teaspoon of salt
¼ teaspoon of Worcestershire sauce
Dash of pepper

Mix egg and tomato sauce thoroughly. Add in remaining ingredients except the bacon. Mix thoroughly and form into 16 rolls about 2 inches long. Wrap each with a half slice of bacon and secure with a toothpick. Broil 5 inches from heat for 8 to 10 minutes. Turn often to brown evenly.

CRISPY BACON OYSTERS

12 ounces of drained oysters
10 slices of bacon cut in half
2 tablespoons of parsley
Salt and pepper

Place oyster on a piece of bacon and sprinkle with parsley, salt and pepper. Wrap bacon around oyster and secure with a toothpick. Repeat. Broil 8 minutes on one side, flip and broil 5 minutes on the other side.

FIESTA BURGER

1 pound of ground beef
8 slices of bacon
1 cup of crushed cornflakes
1 cup of diced tomatoes
1 egg
1 small onion, diced
1 teaspoon of salt
¼ teaspoon of pepper
4 hamburger buns

Mix beef, cornflakes, tomato, egg, salt and pepper. Form into 4 patties. Wrap 2 slices of bacon around each patty. Broil, grill or bake 7 to 10 minutes per side.

FISH STEW

5 pounds of walleye (or similar fish)
3 quarts of water
2 cans of tomatoes
3 chopped onions
3 potatoes, diced
4 hard boiled eggs, diced
4 strips of bacon, diced
½ stick of butter
1 large can of tomato paste
1 tablespoon of Worcestershire sauce
Tabasco to taste

Cover fish with water and boil until tender. Remove fish, add all the ingredients and simmer for one hour. Bone the cooked fish and add to stew for the last five minutes of cooking.

GLAZED BACON

1 pound of bacon
1 cup of brown sugar

Cut bacon strips in half and let rest until they reach room temperature. Dip the strips into the brown sugar. Bake strips on an oven rack at 300 degrees for 45 minutes. Put foil or baking sheet underneath the bacon to catch the drippings. You can also cook the bacon in the broiler. Remove from oven, drain on paper towel and let cool.

GREAT WHITE NORTH BACON SOUP

2½ quarts of boiling water
16 ounces of half & half
½ pound of bacon, fried and crumbled
1 onion, diced fine
12 ounces of Cheez Whiz
½ teaspoon of liquid smoke (optional)
¾ cup of flour
2 cups of Cheddar cheese, grated
8 chicken bouillon cubes
2 carrots, diced fine
1 stick of butter
Salt and pepper to taste

Sauté carrots and onion in butter. Add in flour to make a paste. Drop bouillon cubes in boiling water. Add bouillon and paste mixtures together. Keep stirring to keep it smooth and free of lumps. Add remaining ingredients and season to taste. Simmer for 1 hour.

HOT BACON & CHEESE DIP

8 strips of bacon, diced
8 ounces of cream cheese, cubed
2 cups of Cheddar cheese, shredded
6 tablespoons of Half & Half
1 teaspoon of Worcestershire sauce
¼ teaspoon of dry mustard
¼ teaspoon of onion salt
Dash of Tabasco sauce

Fry bacon in a skillet until crisp then drain on paper towels. Put cream cheese, Cheddar cheese, Half & Half, Worcestershire sauce, mustard, onion salt and Tabasco sauce into a slow cooker. Mix the ingredients thoroughly. Cook on low for 1 hour and allow cheese to melt slowly. 10 minutes before serving, stir in the bacon.

HAM & BACON FRIED RICE

6 slices of bacon
½ onion, chopped
6 carrots, sliced and diced
3 celery stalks, sliced and diced
2 cups of cubed ham
2 scrambled eggs
2 cups of cooked rice

Fry bacon, remove and crumble. In the drippings, sauté onion until tender then add carrots, celery and ham. Cover and cook until tender. Stir in rice. Add bacon and scrambled eggs a few minutes before serving.

HEART STOPPING WEENIES

1 package of Hillshire Farms Lil Smokies
1 pound of bacon
½ cup of brown sugar
Toothpicks

Cut bacon into pieces big enough to wrap around weenies and sugar with a toothpick. Top each one with ½ teaspoon of brown sugar. Put them on a cookies sheet and bake for 20 minutes at 400 degrees. When serving, keep a cardiologist's phone number handy just in case.

HUNTERS FEAST

1 pound sliced bacon
1½ pounds of raw ham, cubed
1 large can of tomato puree
1 large can of whole kernel corn
1 can of lima beans
1 can of mushrooms
1 package spaghetti
2 large onions

Cut bacon slices in half and fry. Fry cubed ham in bacon fat. Fry sliced onion until golden brown. Cook spaghetti as to package directions. Combine all ingredients. Bake at 350 degrees for 60 to 75 minutes.

NORTHWEST PASSAGE CHOWDER

    6 slices of bacon, in pieces
    1 onion, diced
    1 stalk of celery, finely chopped
    ¼ cup of green pepper, finely chopped
    2 large potatoes, cleaned and diced
      (soaked in salt water)
    12 ounces of chopped clams (reserve liquid)
    12 ounces of clam juice
    1 tablespoon of flour
    1 teaspoon of salt
    ½ teaspoon of black pepper
    3 pints of half & half
    1 teaspoon of file` powder
    ½ teaspoon of dried thyme
    Dash of cayenne pepper (optional)

Cook bacon in a large pan, than add onion, celery and green pepper. Sauté until vegetables are soft. Add cubed potatoes and drain. Mix clam juice, flour and salt together and stir into vegetables. Simmer until potatoes are tender. Add clams. Stir in half & half and seasonings. Heat until hot, shy of boiling.

NUTS & BACON

2 cups of mixed nuts
4 slices of bacon, cooked and crumbled
2 tablespoons of brown sugar
2 teaspoons of Cajun seasoning
1 egg white

Beat egg white until foamy. Mixed thoroughly with nuts, sugar, seasoning and bacon crumbles. Bake on a cookie sheet at 325 degrees for 10 to 12 minutes.

QUACKER AND BACON

1 duck (cleaned)
1 apple
¼ peeled onion
6 slices of bacon
2 orange slices
¼ cup of water
Salt and pepper

Salt and pepper inside of duck to taste. Cut apple into quarters and place inside cavity along with onion. Put the duck in a roasting pan and place bacon slices on top of duck. Cover with aluminum foil and cook at 350 degrees for 2 hours. Reduce heat to 300 degrees and cook for an additional 2 hours. If the duck is not browning, remove foil and carefully add water to the roaster. Stick orange slices to the breast with toothpicks and serve.

SPLIT PEA SOUP

½ pound of bacon
5 cups of water
1 cup of milk
10 ounces of split peas (dry)
1 carrot, chopped
1 teaspoon of salt

In a large pan, cook bacon on medium heat. Remove bacon when done and drain the grease. Combine water and split peas in the pan. Simmer on medium uncovered for 45 minutes. If mixture gets too thick, add a little more water. Stir in carrots and bacon and simmer for 20 more minutes. Stir in milk and salt and heat until piping hot.

STUFFED MUSHROOMS

Mushrooms, fresh about 1 to 2 inches in size
5 tablespoons of bacon, crumbled or bits
3 green onions, chopped
8 ounces of softened cream cheese
½ cup of cheddar cheese

Wash mushrooms and remove stems. Place upside down on a cookie sheet. Chop stems. In a bowl mix stems, bacon, green onion and both cheeses. Spoon the mixture into mushroom caps. Bake at 350 degrees for 15 minutes.

SWEET & SPICY BACON

    1 pound of bacon
    Brown Sugar
    Chili powder

Sprinkle chili powder of your choice onto the raw bacon slices. Now press slices into brown sugar. Place a baking rack on a cookie sheet. Line up bacon strips on the rack but don't let them touch. Put the rack and cookie sheet in the oven and bake at 350 degrees for 18 to 20 minutes, turn slices once at the halfway point.

TROUT WITH AN OINK

1 pound of bacon
2 onions, thinly sliced
2 fresh trout, cleaned
½ cup of corn meal
½ cup of flour
1 tablespoon of salt
1 tablespoon of pepper

Fry bacon and remove once it is crisp. Sauté onions in the bacon grease. Remove onions and lightly salt. Mix corn meal, flour, salt and pepper thoroughly and coat fish with the mixture. Fry fish in the grease until done and very crisp. Garnish with fried onion and bacon.

TWISTED BACON

20 slices of bacon
½ cup of packed brown sugar
3 teaspoons of ground mustard
¼ teaspoon of cinnamon
¼ teaspoon of nutmeg
Pinch of cayenne pepper

Combine ingredients and mix thoroughly. Rub mixture over the bacon. Twist the slices and place on a baking rack in a roasting pan or on a cookie sheet. Bake at 350 degrees for 25 to 30 minutes or until meat is firm.

VENISON BACON BURGERS

1 pound of ground venison
1 pound of ground chuck
8 strips of bacon
4 slices of American cheese
4 ounces of mushrooms, fresh or canned
½ onion, diced
2 tablespoons of butter
Garlic powder
Salt and pepper

Mix venison and ground chuck to form 8 large, thin patties. Sauté onion in butter. Place a slice of cheese, onion, mushrooms and seasoning on 4 of the patties. Top with a second patty and pinch the edges together forming a "stuffed" burger. Wrap the patties in 2 crisscross strips of bacon and secure with a toothpick. Cook over medium-hot coals for about 10 minutes or bake at 375 degrees for 8 to 12 minutes, depending on desired doneness.

WILD RICE & BACON SOUP

½ cup of wild rice
1 pound of bacon
¾ cup of celery, chopped
1 cup of onion, chopped
¼ cup of green bell pepper, chopped
28 ounces of chicken broth
4 ounces of mushrooms, canned
3 cans of cream of mushroom soup

Wash rice. Boil for 15 minutes, drain and set aside. Fry bacon until crisp. Sauté celery, onion and green pepper in 3 tablespoons of bacon grease. When onion turns translucent, put sautéed vegetables, bacon, rice, broth, mushrooms and soup into a large pot. Cook on low heat for at least 1 hour. If soup is too thick, add a little more broth.

For more information on the entire series of Tim Murphy's "Cookbooks for Guys" and his other book projects, visit www.flanneljohn.com.